YOUR KNOWLEDGE HAS VALUE

Bibliographic information published by the German National Library:

The German National Library lists this publication in the National Bibliography; detailed bibliographic data are available on the Internet at http://dnb.dnb.de .

Imprint:

Copyright © 2012 GRIN Verlag
Print and binding: Books on Demand GmbH, Norderstedt Germany
ISBN: 9783656710370

This book at GRIN:

https://www.grin.com/document/277880

Laura Herrmann

Summary E-Commerce

GRIN Verlag

GRIN - Your knowledge has value

Since its foundation in 1998, GRIN has specialized in publishing academic texts by students, college teachers and other academics as e-book and printed book. The website www.grin.com is an ideal platform for presenting term papers, final papers, scientific essays, dissertations and specialist books.

Visit us on the internet:

http://www.grin.com/

http://www.facebook.com/grincom

http://www.twitter.com/grin_com

- 2 computers connected by telephone cable (internet was born)
- roots in the cold war
- 1957 Soviet Union launched first satellite (Sputnik I) -> US President Dwight Eisenhower created ARPA agency to regain technological lead in the arms race
- Licklider = head new IPTO organization (help protect US against a space-based nuclear attack)
- Licklider promoted within the IPTO idea of country-wide communications network
- Lawrence Roberts implemented his vision
- Development of a special computer -> ARPANET (Advanced Research Projects Agency Network), October, 1969
- first communications between Leonard Kleinrock's (research center in LA) and Douglas Engelbart (research center in Stanford)
- 1983 ARPANET split into
  - „normal internet
  - military network (MILNET)
- ARPANET provided good communication links between major computational resources, computer users in academic, industrial, and government research laboratories
- 1990 ARPANET was retired and transferred to the NSFNET (National Science Foundation)
- NSFNET soon connected to CSNET (linked Universities around North America), then to the EUnet (connected research facilities in Europe)
- use of the Internet exploded after 1990
- first commercial internet provider started in 1990
- 1991 internet introduced to the public
- US Government transferred management to independent organizations starting in 1995
- In Germany:
  - developed at the universities of Karlsruhe and Dortmund
  - August 1984: first node established at the university Karlsruhe (allowed to communicate with US & other countries per e-mail)
  - 1988: First connection at the university Dortmund into the american internet
  - Small independent providers are main reason for the spread of internet in the beginning

2. Difference between www and Internet / Who invented www

Internet	WWW
global system of interconnected computer networks	one part of the internet
global data communications system	system of interlinked hypertext documents
hardware and software infrastructure that provides connectivity between computers	one service conveyed via the internet

- www was developed by Tim Berners-Lee (member of CERN) in 1989
- 30 April 1993: Tim Berners-Lee presents HTML (the „language of the internet) the first browser as well as the first site on the www for free public use.

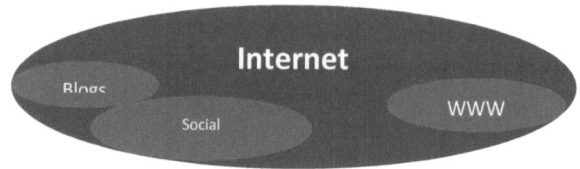

3. Typical services of www

Basic Services (e-mail is best known service for exchange of information)	Bulletin Board Services (Platforms and discussion panels)	Information Services (Search for information on the internet)
eMail	Usenet (Newsgroups)	World Wide Web
Telnet	Listserv	Archie
FTP File Transfer Protocol	Mailinglists	Gopher
		WAIS
		HyTelnet

4. Technical background (what inventions, how many listeners)
   - To reach 50 Mio people in the USA:
     - Radio: 38 years
     - TV: 13 years
     - WWW: 5 years
   - Facebook added 50 million users in just three months
   - Immense increase of the diffusion speed over the last 80 years

     -

5. New Economy
   - = the impact of information technology on the economy
   - Everyone wanted to be a part in the new economy (every business thought they cannot do without being part of the eBusiness and eCommerce)
   - grew very fast, everyone invested (even old economy companies) but without a plan, strategy, etc.
   - eventually "imploded"
   - people underestimated impacts which new technical advances bring along
   - also known as "Digital Economy"
   - developed in the late 90s
   - banks gave loans easily which resulted in a big number of business start ups
   - traditional measures of value no longer valid because technology was changing the world quickly and dramatically
   - "gain market share at all cost"
   - Venture Capital Companies invested millions in .com ideas -> Stock shares rose dramatically
   - recession of 2001 disproved many of the more extreme predictions made during boom years
   - speculative bubble with climax on March 10, 2000
   - „dot-com" bubble:
     - companies lived in a bubble. → after 1 year bubble exploded
     - many companies failed
     - many had to change names to create a new Brand Identity or went totally bankrupt
     - dismissal of employees
     - after 18 months people regain trust and invest again in .com companies
     - after 10 years of the NASDAG crash people seem to have forgotten about it → nowadays another tendency to invest a lot of money in .com market
     - Could this happen again?
       - harder for people to trust in impersonal companies, e.g. google, amazon,…
       - very changing market, every 6 months new technology, new trends -> makes people unsure

- don't know who can see all your information, who can use it & what they'll do with

6. Some Definitions
- eCommerce
  - is a subset of ebusiness, is the purchasing, selling, and exchanging of goods and services over computer networks (such as the Internet) through which transactions or terms of sale are performed electronically
- eBusiness
  - is the transformation of key business processes through the use of Internet technologies
  - wo main ways within organizations:
    - applied to strategies and operations (our organization needs an improved e-business strategy)
    - used as an adjective to describe business that mainly operates online
- relationship e-commerce / e-business:
  - eCommerce has some degree of overlap with eBusiness
  - eCommerce is broadly equivalent to eBusiness
  - eCommerce is a subset of eBusiness

7. B2C /B2B/C2B/C2C

	Consumer	Business
Consumer	Consumer –to-Consumer (C2C) • eBay • Peer-to-Peer (Skype) • Blogs/communities • Product recommendations social networks (Bebo, Facebook, MySpace)	Business-to-Consumer (B2C) • Transactional: amazon • Relationship-building: BP • Brand-building: Unilever • Media owner: News Corp • Comparison intermediary: Kelkoo, Pricerunner
Business	Consumer -to-Business (C2B) • Priceline • Consumer-feedback, communities or campaigns	Business-to-Business (B2B) • Transactional: Euroffice • Relationship-building: BP • Media owner: Emap business productions • B2B marketplace: EC21 social networks (Linkedin, Plaxo)

8. What is Intranet / Extranet?

- Intranet:
  - = a private network within a single company using the Internet standards to enable employees to access and share information using web publishing technology
- Extranet:
  - = a service provided through the Internet and web technology delivered by extending an intranet beyond a company to customers, suppliers and collaborators

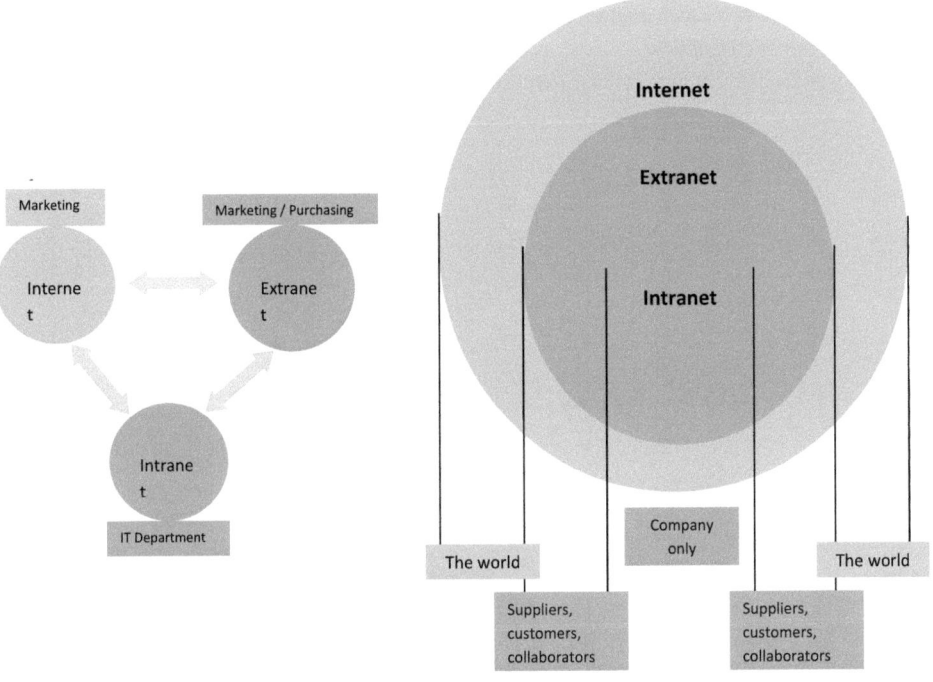

9. Information Society
   - development into an information society since 1990s due to speed of information available
   - nowadays computers made for everyone, not exclusive to the professional
   - some time ago - people were consumers of physical products
   - today - information is our main product (intangible)
   - information society:
     - Physical World
     - Virtual World
   - willingness to pay for information
   - we want to see s.th. or listen to s.th.
   - information overflow
   - starting point of net economy (=an economy created by the usage of the Internet)

10. Five key drivers

- Development of computer performance
  - basis: Performance capacity of computers
  - exponential growth in computer performance, decline in hardware costs
  - Moore's Law
- The power of digitalization
  - processing large amounts of text & pictures quickly & without a quality loss
  - biggest problem of digitalization: data compression
- Increasing Networking
  - everyone can participate in electronic communication
  - new forms of communication, globalization, no special restrictions, increasing speed of information exchange
  - currently impossible to predict final form of the internet
  - crucial factors: availability, speed (!), costs
- The increasing amount of data
  - information becomes separate economic sector
  - basis = ependence on numbers & performance of hardware
  - transfer normal business life into the network
  - business processes changed from personal level to global data networks
  - problem: not possible to use all the information (information becomes competitive factor)
- Relevance of information
  - Crucial parameters:
    - Earlier: product features (quality), conditions (price)
    - Today: speed & flexibility
    - Information becomes a separate competitive factor (produce & receive information more simply & quickly)

11. Moore's law
- observation made in 1965 by Gordon Moore, co-founder of Intel
- = every 18 months speed of processors will double

12. Web 2.0

- = participate, be active, have an interactive part, web as a platform
- Tim O'Reilly (2005): „Like many important concepts, Web 2.0 doesn't have a hard boundary, but rather, a gravitational core. You can visualize Web 2.0 as a set of principles and practices that tie together a veritable solar system of sites that demonstrate some or all of those principles, at a varying distance from that core".
- no real existing definition
- not a new invention but a proceeding realization of the original objective of the network of people (only a new system and way to use it)
- concept leans on versions of the software products
- users create, publish & share contents
- users are connected by social networks
- no longer dominated by large media companies
- includes Internet applications and platforms which integrate the user actively into the value added
- classification:
  - o Communities: build friendships with others, high social context → MySpace, Friendster
  - o Entertainment providers: entertainment in the foreground → Flickr, YouTube, last.fm
  - o Information providers: self-generated content CMS → Blogs, Wikipedia
- Why Web 2.0 so popular
  - o Better availability (New technologies which enable a clearly simplified usage of the Internet)
  - o Technological infrastructure (Distribution of broadband access to the Internet → Users can access from almost anywhere)
  - o User behavior (The users of the new generation are used to dealing with computers and the Internet)
- Problems:
  - o Content difficult to control
  - o Companies as senders have to except the loss of control
    - ▪ the message of an advertisement may be diluted or destroyed
    - ▪ higher control affects negatively customers' willingness to participate
  - o Massive commercialization of successful web-offers is difficult (i. e. MySpace)
  - o Cost intensive to maintain channels
  - o bad profit margin of many offers in the Web 2.0
  - o target: to find right amount of sociality for users & economic attraction for companies

13. Comparing services of Web 1.0 and Web 2.0

Web 1.0	Web 2.0
Static homepages	Social networks
DoubleClick Web 1.0	GoogleAdsense Web 2.0
offers merchandising for static homepages	based on semantic search words of users
merchandises classic advertising space such as banners etc	context-dependent marketing and a higher probability to succeed
Page view (billing for a number of users)	billing based on the amount of clicks on the ad that brings visitors to the advertiser's website (Cost per click).
Page views	"Cost per click"
Britannica	Online Wikipedia
Content Management	Wikis – temporal and spacial spread authors can create and share documents together
Directories (taxonomy)	Tagging ("folksonomy")
Mp3.com users were able to download music.	Napster no more a central website, rather a Peer-to-Peer-offer. Users were simultaneously suppliers of music files.
Akamai	BitTorrent
Personal websites	Blogs, Social Networks
Publishing	Participation
Screen scraping	Web Services
Stickiness	Syndication

➔ Web 2.0 is no technological innovation but rather a new behavior of the Internet users

14. Push & Pull Communication

- Former communication model:

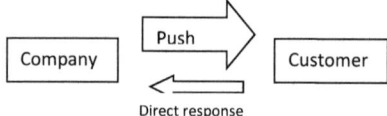

  - Traditional TV, print, radio media & direct mail communication
  - Usual marketing, well-known, repeat message ("Buy Valensina")
  - to create a greater awareness of the brand through advertisement
  - problem: only little or none response possibilities, only through direct feedback

- Modern communications model:

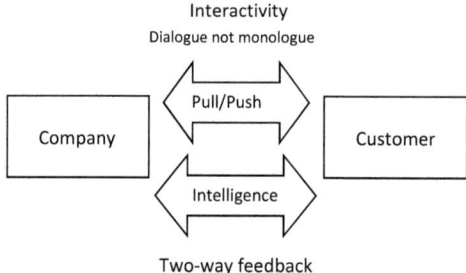

  - companies can receive immediate feedback from customers through blogs, Websites etc.
  - advertisement message fits to interests
  - problem: companies could lose control of their brand

15. 1-2 mega trends

- The death of control
  - The age of control
    - Big organizations had a monopoly on mass communication and got used to controlling the message
  - The age of influence
    - Anyone literate with an internet connection can self-publish for free
    - It is very hard to control: we can only influence
- Fragmentation
  - A few centralized channels
    - People got most information from a handful of news media
    - Organizations could efficiently manage (or at least monitor)
    - E.g. easy to realize all media appearance of a company
    - Easy to tackle
  - A huge cloud of interaction
    - Conversations are distributed wherever people form opinions (blogs, social networks, YouTube)
    - Most communication happens not in open but privately owned space (loose control)

16. Attributes of value added

- interactivity (there is always a many-to-many communication)
- dynamic (it is changing fast)
- decentralization (everyone can use it, no rules what to upload, democratic)

17. Revenue sources

- Advertising
  - success factors:
    - Profiling the users
    - possibility to link the ad to the dependence on the user preferences
    - high coverage and high user rates
    - ensuring that the environment in which the ad is shown cannot damage the advertiser's reputation
  - best known source of revenue
  - more target-oriented as in the classic media
  - context-oriented ads and contents
  - in the future: reference to user profile
- Charges
  - success factors:
    - profiling the users
    - prevention of migration of the users by incompatibility to other offers and high data/information quality
    - high coverage in the focused target group
    - data must be in a form that provides relevant information to the user
  - charging models slowly established (people consider information to be free of charge)
  - requirements:
    - clear offer
    - explicit and strong benefit for a specific target group
  - high coverage important
  - customer loyalty fundamental
  - examples: XING and LinkedIN (basic membership costless - Premium costs)
- Cross-Selling
  - already established in the Internet
  - particularly shopping and tourism providers use this
  - requirement: profiling the users to satisfy his expectations and needs
  - Example: Amazon suggests other articles during the buying process

➜ Best to use sources (coverage more important than revenue)

18. Social media (criteria)

- = a category of sites that is based on user participation and user-generated content
- includes
  - social networking sites like LinkedIn or Facebook
  - social bookmarking sites like Del.icio.us
  - social news sites like Digg or Reddit
  - other sites that are centered on user interaction
- = media that is posed by the user and can take many different forms
- types:
  - forums
  - message boards
  - blogs
  - wikis
  - podcasts
- = software tools that allow groups to generate content, engage in peer-to-peer conversations and exchange of content (examples are YouTube, Flickr, Facebook, MySpace, etc.)
- advertisements formerly based on AIDA principle - nowadays social media give the possibility to transmit information faster
- typical criteria of social media:
  - Collaborate (Participants are asked to provide input and feedback – approach between media and audience)
  - Openness (Social media is about cooperation and open exchange of information. Anyone can join, there are no access restrictions)
  - Entertainment (Social media are built on dialogue and listening)
  - Community (Social media enable like-minded people to come together quickly and toform communities)
  - Connection (Social media is networking. They make use of links to other sites, resources and people)

19. Small world (what is the idea? Where used?)
- = a social-psychological concept by Stanley Milgram (1967) about social networking of the modern society
- Hypothesis:
  - everyone only a few steps away from any other person on Earth
  - chain of „a friend of a friend" statements can be made to connect any two people (Information packets were sent to 60 randomly selected individuals and basic information about the target person in Boston. If they knew the target personally, they had to send the packet directly to him. If they didn't know the target personally, they had to forward the packet to a friend who was more likely to know the target. Three packets reached the target person. The average path length was around 5,5.)
- phenomenon observable in online networks (onnections between people shown directly)
- social communities websites like (XING, Friendster, MySpace, Orkut, Cyworld, Bebo, Facebook etc.) have greatly increased the connectivity of the online space through the application of social networking concepts

20. Storytelling
- reasons for success:
  - authenticity
  - interpretative flexibility
  - word-of-mouth marketing
- problems:
  - brand is in the background
  - campaign tends to get more successful BUT not predictable how successful it is going to be → you may lose control
- make people identify themselves with a story
- good story: dramaturgy (Challenge: tell story in 30 seconds for advertisement)

21. Viral Marketing (+ examples)
- word-of-mouth
- recommendations on websites
- contagious, curiosity → can´t say no to it
- possibilities such as RSS and Widgets (i. e. in blogs).
- possibility for an invitation to the community as next opportunity
- considered more acceptable than an advertisement
- connecting user to the further development of the offer (feedback of the users about the functions or features)
- needs a strategy, concept and good story (-> storytelling)

22. Marketing in eCommerce

- Development in the US in 1950s
- shift from market of demand to market of supply
- holistic approach
- 4 P's
  - Product : emphasis on product /real product innovations, no competition/Monopoly
  - Price: price aggressive market strategy
  - Place: online distribution, no shops, no time and geographical limits
  - Promotion: no product differences compared to competitor products, large budget on advertising, long term communication strategy
  - Today promotion more important than product
- Philip Kotler: "Marketing is not the art of finding clever ways to dispose of what you make. It is the art of creating genuine customer value."
- The old rules of Marketing
  - Marketing simply meant advertising
  - Advertising needed to appeal to the masses
  - Advertising relied on interrupting people to get them to pay attention to a message
  - Advertising was one-way: company-to-consumer
  - Advertising was exclusively about selling products
  - Advertising was based on campaigns that had a limited life
  - Creativity was deemed the most important component of advertising
- The new rules of Marketing
  - Marketers must shift their thinking from the short head of mainstream marketing to the masses to a strategy of targeting vast numbers of undeserved audience via the web
  - You are what you publish
  - People want authenticity, not spin
  - People want participation, not propaganda
  - Instead of causing one-way interruption, marketing is about delivering content at just the precise moment the audience needs it
- Marketing in social media:
  - majority of businesses (over 80%) reported increase in attention and exposure for their businesses, with small business owners reporting the greatest benefit
  - have to know how to do it
  - not a substitute for traditional marketing, but a complement
  - old media & new media need each other

Traditional Marketing	Social Marketing
Shout out loud	Listening then whisper
About the company: Me, me, me	About the community
Push the product	Pull people with a story
Advertisements for the masses	Target the niches consumes
Control	Open exchange
Nurture: Leads	Nurture and let it grow
PR 1.0: Content is King	Integration of the consumer/ feedback
Interruptive	Deliver useful content at the right time